A DVD-based study series
Study Guide

A FRAGILE STONE

Peter: Jesus' Friend

daylight™
Bible Studies

A DVD-based study series
Study Guide

A FRAGILE STONE

Peter: Jesus' Friend
With Michael Card

Eight Lessons for Group Exploration

DISCOVERY HOUSE
PUBLISHERS®

Feeding the Soul with the Word of God

**The DayLight Bible Studies are based on programs produced by
Day of Discovery, a Bible-teaching TV production of RBC Ministries.**

© 2009 by Discovery House Publishers

Discovery House Publishers is affiliated with RBC Ministries,
Grand Rapids, Michigan.

Requests for permission to quote from this book should be directed to:

Permissions Department
Discovery House Publishers
P.O. Box 3566
Grand Rapids, MI 49501

All Scripture quotations, unless otherwise indicated are taken from the
HOLY BIBLE, NEW INTERNATIONAL VERSION®. NIV® Copyright © 1973, 1978,
1984 by International Bible Society. Used by permission of Zondervan.
All rights reserved.

Study questions by Andrew Sloan
Interior design by Sherri L. Hoffman
Cover design by Jeremy Culp
Cover photo by istockphoto.com

ISBN: 978-1-57293-361-3

Printed in the United States of America

09 10 11 12 / / 10 9 8 7 6 5 4 3 2 1

CONTENTS

INTRODUCTION

Your Own Tour Of Israel

Visiting the far-flung countries of the world has a compelling draw on most of us. Who wouldn't love to walk the streets of London and visit Westminster Abbey? Who wouldn't enjoy a stroll down the Avenue des Champs-Elysées in Paris—ending at the Arc de Triomphe? Or who wouldn't revel in the chance to lie on the sandy shores of the Caribbean Sea in Jamaica or Aruba or St. Martins?

But for most people of faith, there is one travel destination that ranks first on their bucket list of places they would love to visit: Israel. It is there that believers can walk the same roads that Jesus walked, sail the same sea that He tamed, and visit the same Jerusalem that is the center of Christianity's most important events—past and future.

While not all of us can do that—given the variables of budgetary restraints, Middle East conflict, and the shortness of time—perhaps the next best thing is to visit Israel vicariously through someone we know and trust.

For this video Bible study series, we have just the person to do that for you: Michael Card.

Michael traveled to Israel with the *Day of Discovery* video team so they could put together a fascinating series of lessons about the key events and important places in the life of a close friend of Jesus Christ: Simon Peter.

As a result, we have an eight-part series of lessons that will give you a "you are there" feeling about the Holy Land and the interaction between Jesus and Peter. You will visit some of the locales the New Testament tells us about, and you will gain valuable insights into the relationship between the Savior and this fisherman-turned-disciple.

In addition, because this is Michael Card the musician, you will also be able to enjoy some music Michael wrote and produced for the program. Then, after viewing each lesson, you will have an opportunity to think through some of the facts and issues Michael presents in his lessons.

So grab a pencil, sit back, and enjoy Israel as you may have never experienced it before. You won't have to go through security for this visit to the most remarkable piece of real estate in the world.

—Dave Branon
Editor

Getting To Know Peter

DAYLIGHT PREVIEW

Jesus' Land

Imagine what it would feel like to visit the actual places where Jesus conducted His ministry when He was in the area of the Sea of Galilee. In your mind's eye, gaze across that famous body of water. What events come to mind? What characteristics of Jesus stand out as you think of Him ministering in this part of Israel's geography? Which of these places connects with something you know about the Bible story: Capernaum, Bethsaida, Magdala?

—————— COME TOGETHER ——————
Icebreaker Questions

1. Who is your best friend? What could someone learn about you by getting to know that person?

2. Peter's given name was *Simeon* (Hebrew) or *Simon* (Greek), which means "the one who hears." Do you know what your name means? Share with the group what you know about your name.

3. What is the most exciting "fish story" you have ever experienced?

FINDING DAYLIGHT

Experience the Video

Feel free to jot down Video Notes as you watch Michael Card's presentation. Use the space below for those notes.

─────────────── VIDEO NOTES ───────────────

Peter's name

Visiting Capernaum

Best friends and Jesus

Fishing on the Sea of Galilee

Facts about Peter

Jesus on board

Jesus' big question

Discussion Time

---------------- DISCOVER GOD'S WORD ----------------

Discussion Questions

1. **In John 1:35–42, Scripture records the occasion when Peter and Jesus first met.**

   a. What emotions do you suppose Peter was feeling after his brother claimed to have found the Messiah (v. 41), and the two of them were walking toward Jesus?

   b. Simon's name went from meaning "one who hears" to "rock" or "stone." How do you think Simon responded when Jesus gave him that new name (*Cephas* in Aramaic, or *Peter* in Greek)?

c. Was Simon Peter already a "rock"? Or was that only to become his destiny in the future? Explain.

2. **The story Michael Card referred to about Jesus' preaching on Peter's boat is found in Luke 5:1–11.**

    a. What do you think went through Peter's mind when Jesus asked to use his boat as a "pulpit" for speaking to the crowd of people?

    b. How might you feel if Jesus showed up at your job and proceeded to tell you how to do your work? Now relate that to Jesus' instructions to Peter that the men should go back out into the deep water and fish again—especially since these career fishermen had fished all night without catching anything.

    c. How did Peter respond to the miraculous catch of fish? What was he afraid of, according to Michael Card? Agree or disagree?

    d. What did Jesus mean when He said to Peter: "Don't be afraid; from now on you will catch men"? How did Peter respond to those words?

LIFE LESSONS

Application Questions

1. Peter's Shared Awareness

What characteristic did Peter share with three great men of the Old Testament?

a.   Genesis 18:27

b.   Job 40:4

c.   Isaiah 6:5

Reflecting on your own life: Thinking about your past or considering your present situation, how can you relate to the principle that drawing nearer to God heightens our awareness of our inadequacy and sinfulness?

Reflecting on your own life: How have you seen this truth work in your life?

2. Jesus' Big Question

Read Matthew 16:13–18. Michael Card points out that when Jesus asked His disciples, "Who do you say I am?" Peter responded by saying more than he knew. In what way was this a defining moment in Peter's life?

Reflecting on your own life: What big question do you think God is asking you at this time in your life?

3. Jesus' Rebuke

Read Matthew 16:21–25. Why did Jesus rebuke Peter?

Reflecting on your own life: How are Jesus' words in verses 24–25 just as relevant to us as they were to Peter and the other disciples?

Reflecting on your own life: What would change in your life if you fully responded to Jesus' call?

DAYLIGHT ON PRAYER

A Time to Share

1. Michael Card states that if Jesus Christ had a best friend it was probably Simon Peter. Peter's faults are well documented, yet Jesus was drawn to Peter. And Jesus profoundly used Peter—a "fragile stone"—in building His church.

   Like Peter, you have the opportunity as a believer and as a group to embark on a journey with Jesus. Share with your group the challenges or obstacles you face in your "friendship" with the Savior. For example, in what way is it hardest for you to obey His call to follow Him? Make this a matter of prayer, with members of the group praying for one another.

2. Also spend some time praying for other important items in your life—the spiritual welfare of others, concerns for others around the world, personal items of praise and prayer.

DAYLIGHT AHEAD

In our next session, we'll join up again with Michael Card as he visits Capernaum, Peter's hometown, to show us around town and to remind us of some important events that Jesus and Peter shared there.

Peter's Home Becomes Jesus' Home

DAYLIGHT PREVIEW

Peter's Homeland

A heavy rainstorm can be fun to experience if you are safely ensconced in your own home and curled up by the fireplace. But storms out on the open sea are something else altogether. Imagine the fear of being on a small fishing boat as waves are crashing, the storm is surging, and rain is pelting down. While Peter was out on the boat in a tempest just like that, he wasn't far from his own place of safety—his mother-in-law's home just down the street from the synagogue—but at the time of the storm fear must have been on his heart.

—— COME TOGETHER ——

Icebreaker Questions

1. What is the most frightening storm you have ever experienced?

2. When have you or a family member encountered a really high fever?

3. What is the most exciting thing that ever happened in your home-town?

FINDING DAYLIGHT

Experience the Video

Feel free to jot down Video Notes as you watch Michael Card's presentation. Use the space below for those notes.

—————————— VIDEO NOTES ——————————

Two storms

Walking on water

Peter: Impetuous or perfect?

Capernaum and the surrounding region

The synagogue

The home of Peter's mother-in-law

Her illness

Peter's ideal woman

WALKING IN THE DAYLIGHT

Discussion Time

—————————— DISCOVER GOD'S WORD ——————————

Discussion Questions

1. **In Mark 4:35–41, we read the story of the storm on the Sea of Galilee.**

    a. How did Peter and the other disciples respond when the storm hit?

    b. How did Jesus respond to the storm? How did He respond to the disciples?

2. **The details of Peter's "walking on water" episode are found in Matthew 14:22–33.**

    a. As Michael Card points out, what effect did the earlier storm have on the way Peter reacted in this situation?

    b. Why is the fact that the disciples worshiped Jesus for the first time the real miracle of this story?

    c. How can you relate to Peter in this story—for example, the way he didn't want to be rebuked again for lack of faith or the way he immediately got out of the boat and walked on the water but then became afraid?

3. **Mark 1:21–34 records Jesus' authority in casting out an evil spirit and healing many sick people.**

    If you were Peter, how would you feel about all the events of this day—especially in light of the fact that they happened not only in your hometown but also in large part in your own home?

LIFE LESSONS

Application Questions

1. Leaving Home

What huge act of faith did Peter and his fishing buddies accomplish as recorded in Luke 5:11?

According to Michael Card, Jesus left home—although under different circumstances. What was significant about Capernaum in relationship to Jesus' departure from Nazareth?

Reflecting on your own life: What move from a home or a community has been the most traumatic or difficult in your life?

2. Leaving It All Behind

When Peter and his friends began to follow Jesus, they left behind the only career track they had ever known. What concerns do you think they had when they did this? Have you ever changed careers? If so, what were your fears?

Reflecting on your own life: Do you need to "leave" anything now in order to follow Jesus completely or more faithfully?

DAYLIGHT ON PRAYER

A Time to Share

1. Pray for one another in light of how group members answered the last question. Commit to continuing to pray for those who recognize a need to "leave" something to follow Jesus more faithfully.

2. As you, like Peter, travel on this journey with Jesus, what other prayer requests would you like to share with your group?

3. Conclude your time together by praying for each other.

DAYLIGHT AHEAD

In our next session, Michael Card reminds us of three new stories from the friendship of Jesus and Peter—stories that will help us to get to know Jesus better.

The Friendship Deepens

DAYLIGHT PREVIEW

Peter's Surprising Friend

Sometimes, friends aren't safe. Have you ever had a friend who pushed the envelope, who challenged the status quo, or who saw things differently from everyone else? Welcome to Peter's world. He has a Friend who makes unorthodox statements and who causes mysterious and miraculous things to happen. Think for a moment what it must have felt like to be hanging out with Jesus as He went about Capernaum doing and saying things no one else could ever do or say.

—————— COME TOGETHER ——————

Icebreaker Questions

1. What is your favorite kind of bread or pastry?

2. What is the highest mountain you have ever climbed?

3. What is your most memorable recollection of paying taxes?

FINDING DAYLIGHT

Experience the Video

Feel free to jot down Video Notes as you watch Michael Card's presentation. Use the space below for those notes.

——————— VIDEO NOTES ———————

The Capernaum synagogue

The bread and the cup

Peter's second confession

The transfiguration

Peter's transformation

Peter's last will and testament

Jesus and taxes

The miracle within the miracle

 WALKING IN THE DAYLIGHT

Discussion Time

———————— DISCOVER GOD'S WORD ————————

Discussion Questions

1. **In John 6:48–66, we read some surprising words from Jesus as He suggests that people will "eat the flesh of the Son of Man and drink His blood."**

   a. What do you think the people must have thought when they heard Jesus say this?

b. What symbolism has to be understood for this passage to be read properly?

2. **Jesus' words caused many to turn away. Read about this in John 6:67–69.**

a. What tone of voice do you imagine Jesus used when He asked the Twelve, "You do not want to leave too, do you?"

b. How does Peter's reply in verses 68–69 demonstrate that Peter accepted Jesus' claim in verse 63?

c. Have you ever been tempted to turn back and no longer follow Jesus? What happened?

d. In light of the possibility of turning away from Jesus, consider the implication of Peter's question: "Lord, to whom shall we go?" (v. 68).

3. **In Mark 9:2–8, the writer explains what must have been one of Peter's most startling events while he was in Jesus' presence.**

   a. What kinds of emotions do you think Peter experienced during this scene?

   b. What does Michael Card mean when he says that this was the *transfiguration* of Jesus, but it was really the *transformation* of Peter? What can we learn about our own spiritual transformation by examining this story?

4. **A fish and a coin play key roles in the tax story of Matthew 17:24–27.**

   How does this story, as Michael Card sees it, illustrate the depth of the friendship Jesus and Peter shared?

─────────────── **LIFE LESSONS** ───────────────

Application Questions

1. **Jesus' Hard Words**

   In John 6:48–66, which we read earlier, Jesus gave what His listeners later called "a hard teaching." His listeners knew the Old Testament, so they knew what Leviticus 17:10–12 said.

   We know that Jesus wasn't talking about eating His flesh and drinking His blood in a literal sense. Jesus was speaking in anticipation of

His crucifixion, when His physical death would become the source of our spiritual life.

Reflecting on your own life: What is the significance of the Lord's Supper in your life? When it takes place at your church, how do you approach it so that it draws you closer to Jesus?

2. Jesus' Sacrifice

Each of us must take the initiative to appropriate the benefits of Christ's sacrifice on our behalf. Jesus calls people to depend on Him for their every need, for their very survival. Those who heard Jesus speak, including many who had been following Him, had trouble with this notion. "This is a hard teaching. Who can accept it? . . . Many of his disciples turned back and no longer followed him" (John 6:60, 66).

Reflecting on your own life: What difference does Jesus—the "Bread of Life"—make in your life? How desperately do you depend on Him as your source of sustenance and strength?

DAYLIGHT ON PRAYER

A Time to Share

1. Like Peter, you can enjoy the miraculous gift of an intimate friendship with Jesus. What obstacles need to be overcome so that the two of you might share an uninterrupted time of fellowship?

2. Spend a minute or two in silent prayer asking God to remove those obstacles.

3. In addition to praying about your relationship with Christ, how else can your group pray for you or your concerns? Conclude your time together by praying for one another.

DAYLIGHT AHEAD

In our next session, Michael Card concludes his time at the Sea of Galilee with a story about a rich man who was afraid to follow Jesus for fear he would have to give up too much.

A Time For Leaving

DAYLIGHT PREVIEW

Leaving Money and Home Behind

It is time for Peter and Jesus to leave the comforts of Galilee behind. As they head for Jerusalem, they'll be walking away from a home, a people, and a culture that is familiar and comfortable. Together, they will be moving into what will turn out to be hostile territory. But before they go, Jesus confronts a rich man about a different kind of leaving—leaving riches in pursuit of true wealth.

Over the past several years, we have seen how temporary riches can be. A faltering world economy has turned rich people into paupers almost overnight. But what happens when Jesus asks a wealthy farmer to voluntarily turn his back on his accumulated riches? Think about what Jesus knew He himself had left behind and what He faced as He asked this well-to-do young man of means to denounce his wealth to follow Him.

COME TOGETHER

Icebreaker Questions

1. Do you know anyone who has come close to giving away everything for Christ?

2. In the video for today, Michael Card will point out that Peter loved to remind Jesus about things. Do you know anyone like that? Could you be that kind of person?

3. Have you ever lived where people thought you had a funny accent? What was that like?

FINDING DAYLIGHT

Experience the Video

Feel free to jot down Video Notes as you watch Michael Card's presentation. Use the space below for those notes.

———————————— VIDEO NOTES ————————————

Jesus and the rich man

Peter's reminder to Jesus

Michael Card's favorite things about the Galilee

Getting ready for Jerusalem

WALKING IN THE DAYLIGHT

Discussion Time

DISCOVER GOD'S WORD

Discussion Questions

1. **In Mark 10:17–27, we read of a conversation between Jesus and a rich young man in which Jesus asked him to leave everything behind.**

   a. How sincere do you think the rich young man was?

   b. Is there any indication that Jesus' instructions in this story were meant to be applied to all Christians? Why or why not?

2. **In the next story, found in Mark 10:28–31, Peter responded to what had just happened with the disappointed rich man.**

   a. Why do you think Peter said, "We have left everything to follow you!" (v. 28)?

   b. How do you think Peter and the other disciples felt about Jesus' reply (vv. 29–31)?

c. In what way was Jesus asking Peter and the other disciples to do something He had already done?

—————————— LIFE LESSONS ——————————
Application Questions

1. **God's Blessings and Riches**

    After the rich man went away sad, Jesus commented, "How hard it is for the rich to enter the kingdom of God!" (Mark 10:23). Michael Card pointed out that these words of Jesus rocked the disciples' world. According to their value system, rich people were wealthy because God had blessed them.

    Reflecting on your own life: How tempted are you to think that material blessings and God's favor go hand-in-hand?

2. **The Question of Salvation**

    The disciples responded by asking, in effect, "Well, who then can be saved, if rich people can't be saved?" Jesus replied, "Humanly speaking, it is impossible. But not with God. Everything is possible with God" (Mark 10:27 NLT).

    Salvation is completely God's doing. Efforts to inherit eternal life on the basis of our own merits or achievements are futile. "For it is by grace you have been saved, through faith—and this not from yourselves, it is the gift of God—not by works, so that no one can boast" (Ephesians 2:8–9). "He saved us, not on the basis of deeds which we have done in righteousness, but according to His mercy" (Titus 3:5 NASB).

Reflecting on your own life: How tempted are you to think that human goodness can earn eternal life?

3. **Giving It Up**

    Peter felt that he and his friends had left "everything" to be Jesus' followers.

    Reflecting on your own life: What have you "left" in order to follow Jesus?

    Reflecting on your own life: How has following Jesus been a mixture of prosperity and persecution for you?

DAYLIGHT ON PRAYER

A Time to Share

1. As Jesus and Peter leave the Galilee behind, they face new challenges. What are some challenges you face as you leave today behind and move into tomorrow? Are there some items that you can share with your group to pray about?

2. What other prayer requests would you like to share with the group?

3. Close by praying for each other.

DAYLIGHT AHEAD

In our next session, we'll visit again with Michael Card as he travels to Jerusalem to visit a re-creation of the Last Supper. There, among the implements
of that important Jewish Passover meal, Card will help us walk through the
personal drama of Jesus' interaction with John, Peter, and Judas.

Dinner With Jesus

DAYLIGHT PREVIEW

The Last Supper

As Jesus sat down with His disciples in Jerusalem in a second-floor room that had been prepared by Peter and his friends for a Passover meal, the Lord and His closest followers were not on the same page mentally. All the disciples knew was that it was time for a religious ritual meal—but Jesus was undoubtedly thinking about the events that would arise after the meal . . . events that would lead to His horrendous death on a cross.

Michael Card has moved from the Galilee to the Holy City in our study of the relationship between Jesus and Peter, and now he takes us to a replica of the room where Jesus shared an important Jewish meal with His closest followers, where He revealed the betrayal of one of them, and where He demonstrated true servanthood. Imagine the drama and the surprises wrapped up in this dinner with Jesus.

COME TOGETHER

Icebreaker Questions

1. Can you remember going to a concert, stage production, or sporting event and having one of the best seats in the house?

2. What is the most menial thing you have to do?

3. Have you ever washed someone's feet? If so, what was that experience like?

FINDING DAYLIGHT

Experience the Video

Feel free to jot down Video Notes as you watch Michael Card's presentation. Use the space below for those notes.

──────────── **VIDEO NOTES** ────────────

Peter and John's pre-supper chores

Peter and John's discussion about greatness

Who sat where at the table?

The betrayal

The footwashing

DISCOVER GOD'S WORD

Discussion Questions

1. **In Luke 22:7–16, we read Dr. Luke's details about the preparations for what we call the Last Supper.**

    How do you think Peter felt about being given the task of making preparations for the Passover meal, particularly—as Michael Card points out—in light of the disciples' tendency to argue about which one of them was the greatest?

2. **After the meal ended on this special night, Jesus did something surprising. He grabbed a towel and a water basin and began washing the disciples' feet, as John describes in chapter 13, verses 1–10 of his book.**

    Why did Peter resist having Jesus wash his feet?

Application Questions

1. Peter and the Foot Washing

Michael Card observes that Peter was trying to defend Jesus' dignity. Having just recently seen Jesus transfigured, Peter was saying, in essence, "I will never allow You to do this. This is not appropriate."

Peter's refusal to let Jesus wash his feet was a denial of who Jesus really is. Jesus is our servant Lord, our servant Savior. He longs to wash our feet with the water of His Word.

Jesus' words and actions pointed to that cleansing, which He provides through His life and death. Jesus also said that His disciples ought to wash each other's feet (John 13:14). Those who are cleansed by Him must live out their cleansing by their humble service for one another.

Reflecting on our own life: How hard is it for you to accept Christ's service for you—that is, the cleansing He has made available to us?

Reflecting on your own life: How hard is it for you to follow Jesus' example by serving others, particularly when that involves the most menial of tasks?

2. The Betrayal

At the Last Supper, Jesus surprised the disciples with news that one of them would betray Him. John describes that scene in John 13:18–30.

Michael Card points out that John, the disciple "whom Jesus loved" (John 13:23), was at Jesus' right hand, the place of the honored guest;

Judas occupied the place of the intimate friend, on Jesus' left; and Peter was at the far side of the table, where the servant normally sat.

Reflecting on the story: How do you suppose Peter felt about this seating arrangement?

Reflecting on your own life: As you think about the possibility of being slighted by a good friend, how can this scene help you to realize that the friend may have had a good reason for his or her action—and that it was not directed at you?

3. **Jesus' Prediction about Peter**

In Luke 22:31–34 we read about another surprise that lies ahead— Peter's coming denial of his friend Jesus.

Reflecting on the story: How do you think Peter felt when Jesus said to him, "Before the rooster crows today, you will deny three times that you know me" (v. 34)?

Reflecting on your own life: When was a time you felt as if you denied Jesus to others? What do you need to do to try to prevent that from happening again?

4. Jesus' Prayer for Peter

As the Last Supper came to a close, Jesus said, "Simon, Simon, Satan has asked to sift you as wheat" (Luke 22:31). The word *you* here is plural; Jesus was referring to all the disciples. But then Jesus turned to Simon Peter and said specifically to him, "But I have prayed for you, Simon, that your faith may not fail" (v. 32). And that's how we know why Peter, the "fragile stone," didn't crumble away completely. His best friend was praying for him.

God's Word tells us that Jesus intercedes on our behalf as well. "Christ Jesus, who died—more than that, who was raised to life—is at the right hand of God and is also interceding for us" (Romans 8:34). "[Christ] is able to save completely those who come to God through him, because he always lives to intercede for them" (Hebrews 7:25).

Reflecting on your own life: How does it make you feel to know that Jesus Christ is interceding for *you*?

 ## DAYLIGHT ON PRAYER

A Time To Share

1. As Peter learned, our journey with Jesus involves a combination of allowing Christ to serve us, finding ways to serve Him, and looking for opportunities to serve others. In what way do you struggle with being committed to all three areas? How can your friends pray for you about that?

2. Do you have other concerns you would like the group to pray about?

3. Serve each other by praying for each other.

 ## DAYLIGHT AHEAD

In our next session, we'll walk with Michael Card through the intense night of prayer by Jesus in the Garden of Gethsemane. We'll revisit Peter's reactions to the events of that night—both in the Garden and later in the courtyard as Jesus faces His accusers.

Crisis In The Garden

DAYLIGHT PREVIEW

Intense Times for Jesus and Peter

Have you noticed that friendships are often refined in life's toughest days? For Jesus and Peter, the most difficult times are here. Beginning in the darkness of the Garden of Gethsemane and moving to the fire-lit glow of a courtyard just outside the home of the high priest, this night would test their relationship on several levels. Can Peter be the prayer-partner Jesus needs? How does Peter respond as hundreds of soldiers invade the Garden? And what goes through his head when he realizes that Jesus faces angry accusers—and he could be implicated in Jesus' dilemma?

COME TOGETHER

Icebreaker Questions

1. When have you been greatly embarrassed because you fell asleep?

2. What relationship in your life has included a lot of correction or rebukes? Were you more on the giving or receiving end of those rebukes?

3. Do you remember the look on your mother's or father's face when you disappointed her or him as a child or teenager?

FINDING DAYLIGHT

Experience the Video

Feel free to jot down Video Notes as you watch Michael Card's presentation. Use the space below for those notes.

―――――――――――― **VIDEO NOTES** ――――――――

Jesus falls

Abba Father

Jesus' battle: The submission prayer

The sleeping disciples

Jesus' third prayer

Peter defends Jesus

Peter's state of mind

The denial and Jesus' look

WALKING IN THE DAYLIGHT

Discussion Time

──────────── DISCOVER GOD'S WORD ────────────

Discussion Questions

1. **In Mark 14:32–36 we read about Jesus' visit to Gethsemane with Peter, James, and John.**

   a. Michael Card says that the Garden of Gethsemane was "where the battle was won." What was the nature of that battle for Jesus?

   b. What is the nature of the battle for us?

2. **As the story continues, we read Mark 14:37–50 about the disciples' sleepiness and about Jesus' arrest.**

   a. It seems as if Peter was continually being rebuked by Jesus, even when he did something he thought was right—such as defending Jesus or His dignity. Here Jesus singled out Peter for falling asleep (Mark 14:37). John 18:10–11 specifies that Peter was the one who struck the high priest's servant with a sword, receiving a rebuke from Jesus as a result. If you were Peter, how would you be feeling about all this?

   b. What do you think about Michael Card's analysis that the moment Peter saw Jesus surrender—especially since he had been raised to believe that the Messiah would never suffer, never serve, and never submit—was the moment that Peter broke?

3. **After the arrest, Jesus was taken to be charged before the Sanhedrin, and Peter was confronted about his alleged friendship with the accused. Mark 14:53–54 and Mark 14:66–72 give us the details.**

   a. What does Michael Card mean when he says that Peter's statement, "I don't know this man" (v. 71) is really more of a matter of despair than of fear?

   b. Does that seem to be a reasonable conclusion to you? Explain.

LIFE LESSONS

Application Questions

What Would Peter Do?

All four gospels tell of the denials of Peter. That was an important message for the early church, because many of the believers were being tempted to deny Jesus as well. They needed to hear this story in Peter's life. If it was possible for the apostle Peter—the "rock"—to deny Christ, then they had to be careful lest they deny Him too.

The resolution of Peter's story also offered assurance that if a believer did fail Jesus amid the fire of persecution, an opportunity for repentance and restoration always remained.

Reflecting on your own life: Do you find the story of Peter's denials to be more *discouraging* or *encouraging*?

Reflecting on your own life: When have you been the most tempted to deny Christ?

DAYLIGHT ON PRAYER

A Time to Share

1. Luke 22:61 tells us that after Peter's third denial, Jesus "turned and looked straight at Peter." How can you relate to Michael Card's song lyrics that say Jesus' "gaze was kindness, but His stare was stone—it could break your heart or somehow make you whole"?

2. What prayer concerns would you like to share with the group?

3. Conclude your time by praying for one another.

DAYLIGHT AHEAD

In the seventh session of our study, Michael Card visits a first-century garden tomb to remind us of the glorious events of resurrection morning—and about Jesus' special concern for His friend Peter. Card moves on to the Western Wall—at the sight of the first-century destruction of the temple—to explain Peter's new reality. And he concludes his lesson back on the Sea of Galilee as he describes a special breakfast Jesus cooked for Peter and the others.

New Realities For Peter

DAYLIGHT PREVIEW

"Go Tell Peter!"

Have you ever considered the resurrection from Peter's perspective? Imagine what was running through his mind on that first Easter morning—when he hadn't even understood that a resurrection was coming. Or think of how special Peter must have felt when he heard that Jesus had asked specifically for him to be told about it. Think of how Peter's dream must have died—and how the resurrection changed everything. And contemplate how Peter felt on the morning Jesus fixed some breakfast for him and his freinds back by the Sea of Galilee.

—— COME TOGETHER ——
Icebreaker Questions

1. When you were a kid, what was your best subject in school? What subject did you just not get?

2. Have you ever been in an Easter play? What part did you play?

3. Can you recall seeing someone whose appearance had changed drastically since the last time you had seen him or her?

FINDING DAYLIGHT

Experience the Video

Feel free to jot down Video Notes as you watch Michael Card's presentation. Use the space below for those notes.

—————————— VIDEO NOTES ——————————

Surprise at the tomb

Luke's details about Peter and John

Mark's description—a special word for Peter

The Western Wall

Peter's new reality

The pain of Peter's experience

Breakfast by the sea

 WALKING IN THE DAYLIGHT

Discussion Time

————————— **DISCOVER GOD'S WORD** —————————

Discussion Questions

1. **On this side of the resurrection, we celebrate the events of that great Sunday morning. But as Mark 16:1–7 develops, Jesus' friends have no expectations of such a grand celebration.**

   In light of Peter's denials, how significant are the angel's words, "Go, tell His disciples—and Peter—that He is going before you into Galilee" (Mark 16:7 NKJV)?

2. **Suddenly, Jesus' friends faced a confusing, exciting reality. Jesus was not in the tomb—but they still didn't quite understand what it meant. Luke 24:9–12 speaks of this confusion and wonderment.**

    Even though Jesus had told Peter and the other disciples again and again that He would be raised from the dead, why do you think they had no expectation whatsoever that it was going to happen?

3. **The scene moves back to the Sea of Galilee where Peter and his fellow fishermen had returned to their jobs. John 21:1–14 tells of an exciting story reminiscent of one that took place before the resurrection.**

    a. Why do you suppose Peter had returned to fishing?

    b. Although the disciples recognized the miracle, since this was the second miraculous catch of fish (see Luke 5:1–11), they had difficulty recognizing Jesus (as did Mary Magdalene outside the tomb and the two disciples on the road to Emmaus). Why do you think that was the case?

    c. Does the fact that Jesus was waiting on the shore to serve the disciples breakfast make you, like Michael Card, want to fall down and worship Him more than if He had been waiting with legions of angels?

Application Questions

The Death of Peter's Dreams

Peter experienced the death of his dreams of what Messiah would be. Peter thought that the Messiah was someone you prayed for. But in Gethsemane he heard Jesus praying for *him*. Peter thought that the Messiah was someone you would kill for—and even die for. So he jumped into the middle of the crowd at the Garden of Gethsemane and brandished his sword. Peter never dreamed that the Messiah was someone who would die for *him*.

This was a whole new reality. And Peter was caught in the middle of it. He was experiencing the death—the painful death—of an old dream, a legitimate dream. But Jesus was introducing him to a whole new world, a world that Peter could never in his wildest dreams have imagined.

Reflecting on your own life: How has Jesus brought a death to your own personal dreams and an introduction to a wonderful new dream?

Reflecting on your own life: Is there a dream that you need to let go of in order to accept a new idea from God?

DAYLIGHT ON PRAYER

A Time to Share

1. An important part of our journey with Jesus is worship. What really stirs your heart to express your love and devotion to Him?

2. For what concerns would you like the group to join you in prayer?

3. Bring your time together to a close by combining worship and prayer.

DAYLIGHT AHEAD

As Michael Card's study of the friendship between Peter and Jesus concludes, he returns to Jerusalem to put an exclamation point on these important lessons. In the final session, we'll take a fresh look at Jesus' three questions of Peter, we'll listen in to the last conversation between the disciple and his Lord, and we'll find out what stands out to Michael Card as he thinks back over his examination of The Fragile Stone.

Final Lessons For Peter

DAYLIGHT PREVIEW

"Go For It"

Put yourself in Peter's sandals as he and his friend Jesus have their intense after-breakfast conversation by the big lake. Three times Jesus asks a question; three times Peter answers him in earnest. Have you considered this an affirming pep talk, a time for Jesus to tell His friend, "Go for it"? And what about the final give-and-take between these two friends—the one in which Jesus told Peter how the disciple would die. Think about how *that* went for the one called The Rock.

COME TOGETHER

Icebreaker Questions

1. How do you feel when someone repeatedly says the same thing or asks you the same question?

2. What is your favorite comeback story?

3. If you had a choice, would you like to know how you are going to die?

FINDING DAYLIGHT

Experience the Video

Feel free to jot down Video Notes as you watch Michael Card's presentation. Use the space below for those notes.

─────────────── **VIDEO NOTES** ───────────────

The three questions

One final conversation

Lessons for Peter

The voice of a best friend

WALKING IN THE DAYLIGHT

Discussion Time

—————————————— **DISCOVER GOD'S WORD** ——————————————

Discussion Questions

1. **Breakfast was over, and Jesus had some questions for Peter. Well, one question, really, asked three times. Read about it in John 21:15–17.**

   a. Do you think this was essentially another rebuke, in which Jesus asked Peter, "Do you love Me?" three times as a way of giving Peter three opportunities to reaffirm his love for Jesus since he had denied Him three times? Or do you agree with Michael Card that Jesus' tone here was one of pure encouragement and affirmation, because Jesus and Peter had dealt with those denials in an earlier resurrection appearance (mentioned in Luke 24:34 and 1 Corinthians 15:5)?

   b. At any rate, what effect do you suppose this conversation had on Peter?

   c. If you were ever to feel that you had forfeited your right to serve Jesus, what do you think Jesus would say to you in response?

2. **The conversation continued, but it took a far different turn this time. Read John 21:18–19 for the details.**

Why do you think Jesus wanted Peter to know in advance that, like Jesus, Peter would be crucified?

LIFE LESSONS

Application Questions

The Fragile Stone in All of Us

The apostle Peter was indeed a "fragile stone." This term is filled with irony, yet it aptly describes him. We see this contrast played out in Peter's life as he displayed moments of courage followed by spiritual failure.

Michael Card has learned from Simon Peter that even when he fails, he's not disqualified. God can still use him. That's a comforting word. As Michael says, "I've come to realize that my fragileness and my failures are the things that God uses the most. At those times I'm learning to hear Jesus say exactly what He said to Peter: 'Peter, do you love Me? If you do, then press on.'"

Like Peter, we are all "fragile stones." How grateful we can be for Christ's strength that is made perfect in our weakness (2 Corinthians 12:9–10).

Reflecting on your own life: What failure or struggle in your life has taught you the most?

Reflecting on your own life: In what way have you come to realize that your fragileness and your failures are the things that God uses the most?

DAYLIGHT ON PRAYER

A Time to Share

1. Michael Card shares that since going to the Holy Land he had been struggling "to put everything together." He concludes by saying, "And that's when I imagine Jesus telling me, 'It's not always about putting things together. Sometimes it's just about *being* together.' That's the voice of the best friend of Simon Peter. And that's the voice of the Person that I really want to come to know."

   Do you share Michael's desire to know Jesus more intimately? What steps can you take to move in that direction?

2. What have you appreciated the most about this series and about this group? How can the group support you in prayer?

3. As you close in prayer, thank God for each other and for what you have learned and experienced together.

"You are living stones that God is building into his spiritual temple"
—Peter (1 Peter 2:5 NLT).